WASHINGTON, D.C.
OUR NATION'S CAPITAL

This book was made possible with the help of a grant from

⬒ **Bell Atlantic**

WASHINGTON, D.C.
OUR NATION'S CAPITAL

PHOTOGRAPHY BY CAMERON DAVIDSON

TEXT BY EDWARDS PARK

HarperCollinsSanFrancisco
Visual Information Publishing Group

A WINGS OVER AMERICA™ Project
First published in 1994 by HarperCollins *Visual Information Publishers (VIP)*
Copyright © 1994 HarperCollins, Publishers, Inc.
All Photographs copyright © 1994 Cameron Davidson

For HarperCollins *Visual Information Publishers (VIP)*
Publisher: Robert Cave-Rogers
Design Concept: John Bull, The Book Design Company
Design/Production: Melanie Haage
Copyeditor: Barbara Yoder
Photo Editor: Declan Haun

The WASHINGTON, D.C., OUR NATION'S CAPITAL television special and videotape
was produced by KCTS Television, 401 Mercer Street, Seattle, WA 98109.
President: Burnill Clark
Senior Vice President: Walter Parsons
Executive-In-Charge of Production: Elizabeth Brock
Executive Producer: Jeff Gentes

L'Enfant Plan computer enhancement courtesy Library of Congress and U.S. Geological Survey Center

FIRST EDITION

Library of Congress Cataloging-in-Publication Data
Davidson, Cameron, 1955–
        Washington D.C., our nation's capital / photography by Cameron Davidson ; text by Edwards Park.
            p.   cm.
        Includes index.
        ISBN 0-06-263522-0 (pbk.) : $18.00
        1. Washington (D.C.)—Pictorial works.   2. Washington (D.C.)—Description and travel.
        I. Park, Edwards.   II. Title.
F210.D27 1994
975.3—dc20   93-44478
                                                                                      CIP
Printed in Hong Kong

ACKNOWLEDGMENTS

    Many fine guidebooks make life easy for anyone writing about Washington. I found details of its planning in
Rider With Destiny: George Washington, by my old friend Lonnelle Aikman of the *National Geographic,* and of today's
city in *Washington, D.C.: A Smithsonian Book of the Nation's Capital.* As a writer in both places, I trust their facts.
    Margaret Leech describes Lincoln's city in *Reveille in Washington,* while *The Education of Henry Adams*
and W. R. Thayer's *The Life of John Hay* follow its growth. Most helpful of all were my 27 years of working in
Washington, of reading its papers, listening to its gossip, absorbing its legends, exploring its byways, and falling
under its spell.
                                                                —EDWARDS PARK, AUTHOR, NOVEMBER 1993

    Aerial photography requires the support of many people. It is exhilarating and challenging, but safety
must always come first. These are just some of the people who helped me shoot the photographs in this book,
and to them my sincere thanks:
    Mike Garland, Larry Duppstadt, Shawn LeBritton, Jeff LeDonne *(rotary wing aircraft);* Gary Livac, David
Miller, Bruce Landry, Kevin Carpenter *(fixed wing aircraft);* Robert Downey *(RFK Stadium);* Helen Dalrymple,
James Trew, Victoria Hill, Dr. Stephen James *(Library of Congress);* Marja Morris *(National Park Service);* Art Santry
(Trammell Crow); and the staff at Market Square, Mike Langford, Dave Rockwell *(Capital Color).*
                                                            —CAMERON DAVIDSON, PHOTOGRAPHER, NOVEMBER 1993

Below

Columns left over from a renovation of the
U.S. Capitol now embellish the National Arboretum,
a happy spot that lures botanists.

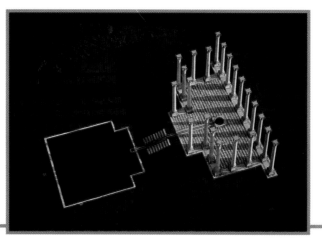

CONTENTS

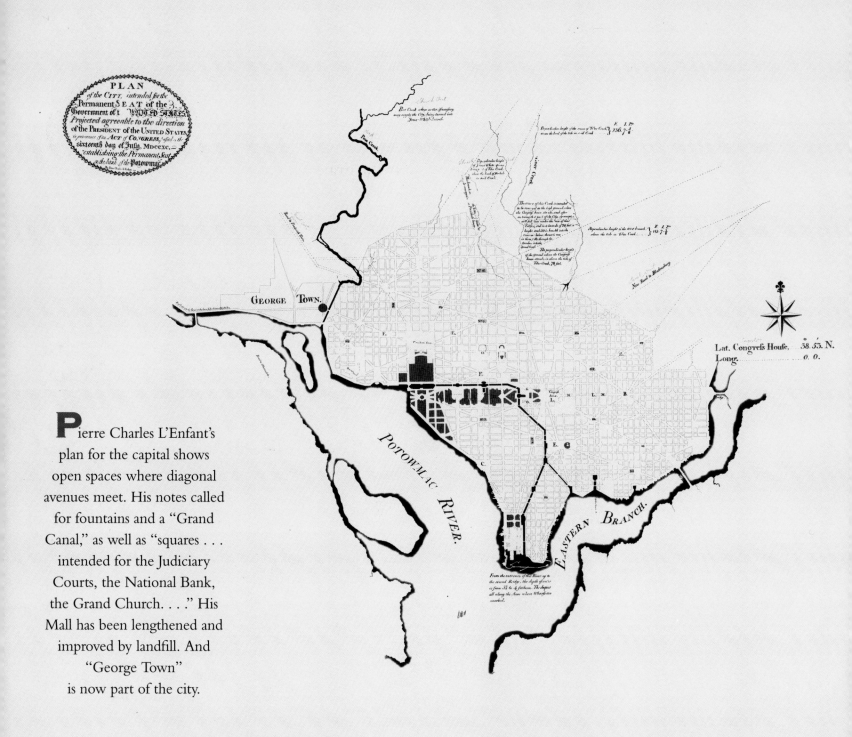

GEORGE TOWN.

POTOWMAC RIVER.

EASTERN BRANCH.

Lat. Congress House, 38. 53. N.
Long. .... 0. 0.

Pierre Charles L'Enfant's
plan for the capital shows
open spaces where diagonal
avenues meet. His notes called
for fountains and a "Grand
Canal," as well as "squares . . .
intended for the Judiciary
Courts, the National Bank,
the Grand Church. . . ." His
Mall has been lengthened and
improved by landfill. And
"George Town"
is now part of the city.

INTRODUCTION

On an evening flight, high above the city, Washington, D.C. may look to you like a giant spray of jewels, a massive, sparkling cascade of lights. It forms a glittering grid, sliced by diagonal ribbons and spotted by circles and squares. Two dark bands form a cross, outlined by five major gems: Three huge baubles—a brilliant high crown, a crystalline spar, and a chaste baguette—lie in a row; at one side gleams a pearl, at the other a diamond.

Spread out so splendidly that it catches your breath, the capital of the United States lies below you. Washington, nucleus of democracy, throne of world power, has become a giant tiara, and it takes you a moment to identify those mighty jewels—the Capitol, the Washington Monument, the Lincoln Memorial, all in line along the darkened Mall; the Jefferson Memorial and the White House on its flanks.

It's a grand spectacle, but it offers only an inkling of the true city. If you could somehow stay aloft, orbiting the capital until dawn, you'd gasp at the sight of your life—the sunrise touching first George Washington's 555-foot obelisk, then the Capitol's towering white dome, by law the city's highest building. Tree shadows would begin to etch streets and avenues, and the Mall would turn green before your eyes, along with the Ellipse, the rim of the Tidal Basin—pink with cherry blossoms in April—and the sinuous forest of Rock Creek Park. Not many American cities can boast such greenery.

Looking down on Washington's heart, you discover its plan: the cardinal avenues, the long vistas, especially the great Mall, stretching through the monumental heart of the city from the Capitol to the Potomac River.

Now morning traffic streams across bridges from Virginia and eastern Maryland and fills the streets. Light increases, and by special dispensation you magically fly low enough, in this book, to look down on the Supreme Court and the Library of Congress, just east of the Capitol and in line with the Mall.

WASHINGTON'S DESIGN

Many Washingtonians think their city is the world's first planned national capital. Actually, Peter the Great built St. Petersburg in Russia as his capital at the beginning of the same century that later saw Washington City begin to rise. But certainly the American example spurred Australia's Canberra and Brazil's Brasilia, and both borrowed ideas from the banks of the Potomac.

From the air it's easy to see how the branches of government are linked in Washington's design. From the Capitol, open parkland sweeps west then turns north (a golfer's dogleg) to the White House. Pennsylvania Avenue, that sheen of gray, by now clogged with traffic, makes the same journey, heading

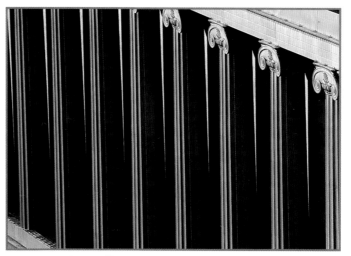

JUSTICE DEPARTMENT, PENNSYLVANIA AVENUE

off straight toward the White House from the Capitol. It was laid out to provide quick and easy communication between president and Congress. No one foresaw, two centuries ago, that despite Pennsylvania Avenue, contact between the two would sometimes totally collapse.

The planning of this noble city began in the minds of eighteenth-century legislators wearied by trundling the government around the whole mid-Atlantic region. During our Revolution and early Federalist days, our capital was, at various times, located in Philadelphia, Pennsylvania, as well as Lancaster and York; in New Jersey (Princeton and Trenton) and Maryland (Baltimore and Annapolis); and New York, where our first president was inaugurated; and finally, back in Philadelphia. No wonder a permanent home, built from scratch, was ever a gleam in the eyes of our Founding Fathers.

They chose the site on the Potomac River—pristine compared to the brown flow you look down on today—through a political deal, the first of thousands to be born on this spot. A French engineering officer, Pierre Charles L'Enfant, who had served under General Washington, finagled the task of town planner.

Like many Europeans, including even a good many British, L'Enfant saw the newborn United States as a fresh garden for human hopes. He visualized a capital for this infant republic that would express mankind's loftiest aspirations. It would be a breathtaking metropolis with room for "aggrandisement & embellishment which the increase in the wealth of the Nation will permit."

George Washington, who insisted on calling the Frenchman "Langfang," tended to go along with his notion of grandeur. Thomas Jefferson, however, saw the United States as an agricultural nation, with a stately but simple capital that would fit into a mere 1,500 acres. Factions formed and, of course, land speculators hung on the outskirts of the great project like jackals eyeing the stalking lions.

L'Enfant lost his job. Other planners took over, amid contention and financial worries. The first buildings of the new capital finally arose out of more compromises, more back-room deals. The city's early growth was so reluctant that Jefferson's notion of it seemed to have won out.

It was indeed a southern village. Everyone who was anybody knew everyone else—and put the considerable discomforts of life out of mind by incessantly partying. Political transients crammed the place annually for a few weeks, then scuttled back home as quickly as possible. Slave pens abutted federal buildings that had been constructed to celebrate the rights of man. The Capitol dome took years abuilding so that entire generations of senators and representatives did their duties without it. Tiber Creek, running along the edge of the Mall, where L'Enfant had hoped for fountains and cascades, became a reeking sewer before it was finally filled, boarded over, buried and forgotten.

FLAWS IN THE CITY PLAN

From the air, you notice a few of the many flaws. Why, for example, isn't the Washington Monument at the exact intersection of the

Mall and the crossing vista between White House and Jefferson Memorial? Answer: Much of the lower Mall is landfill, and the monument, begun at the right spot, began to sink. It was moved to firmer ground.

Why doesn't Pennsylvania Avenue reach straight from the Capitol to the White House as it was supposed to do? Why was it blocked by the U.S. Treasury Building? The answer may or may not be that after burning down twice, the treasury's rebuilding was delayed by arguments over its site until President Andrew Jackson paused during a walk along Pennsylvania Avenue and impatiently banged his cane on the ground. "Have them put it *here!*" he roared at an aide. And they did.

A closer view of Washington spurs more questions: Why isn't Horatio Greenough's classical marble statue of George Washington in the Capitol rotunda where it was designed to fit? Answer: Because it almost fell through the floor. It was moved, finally, to the Smithsonian.

THE CAPITOL

And where is that sacred relic, the Capitol cornerstone, ceremoniously laid in 1793 by the first president in his masonic apron? Embarrassed answer: Somehow it's been mislaid. No one can find it.

The capital has as many such anecdotes as it does lobbyists. But despite all the bumbles, misjudgments, and false starts, it wrenched itself through its distasteful adolescence. Chivvied along by wars, political bosses, visionaries, and occasionally even a statesman or two, Washington has acquired grandeur as well as ghosts. It enters maturity with a distinctive charm.

WASHINGTON UP CLOSE
These pages not only fly you over the city, but land you among its people—First Ladies Abigail Adams and Dolley Madison; Confederate General Robert E. Lee and suffragist Sojourner Truth; naval hero Stephen Decatur and endless swarms of Vietnam veterans at "The Wall"; Teddy Roosevelt's youngsters pedaling tricycles through the White

House while their father skinny-dips in Rock Creek.

Seen closeup, Washington reveals its restless improvements and adjustments. Its residents and commuters sometimes wonder if their city will ever be finished. But then, you could say the same for the United States. For two centuries, Washington has reflected faithfully the democracy whose leadership it houses. It has mirrored our growth, our tragedies, our prosperity, and our kindnesses.

In early days of the Civil War, regiments of young northern troops camped out in public buildings, including the Capitol. A little later many returned, torn and bloody, to the same places, to be nursed by Louisa May Alcott, perhaps, or Clara Barton, and soothed by the gentle poet Walt Whitman.

In the post-war boom, great houses arose along Massachusetts and Connecticut Avenues, elegant dinner parties rang with the brilliant repartee between Secretary

of State John Hay and the great Henry Adams. New art museums and theaters belied the capital's reputation as a cultural desert. In Depression days, war veterans slapped together a shantytown near the Capitol from which to protest their lack of a proper pension. They were finally dispersed by troops under Douglas MacArthur.

Our nation's capital has arisen, like our nation, out of dispute and compromise, somehow welding together soaring ideals and penny-pinching realities, golden dreams and grim awakenings. The city is flawed, just as is democracy itself. But rough edges and all, Washington distills the entire story of the United States: its hopes and disappointments, its addiction to ideals and also to greed, its puffery and its despair, its fumbling of some dreams and its triumphant attainment of others.

Meet a great city that is inadequate, costly, crime-ridden, and sometimes absolutely disgraceful, a city that also reaches for—and sometimes touches—the best that we all can be.

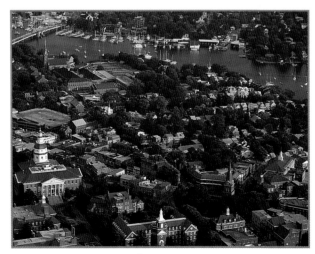
ANNAPOLIS

Part One

THE CAPITAL'S MONUMENTAL HEART

L ike all cities, Washington is a living organism. Head and heart are its great government buildings, its repositories of the republic's ideals and accomplishments, and its monuments and memorials to the extraordinary leaders who first visualized the nation, then shaped it, guided it, and saved it. Here's close scrutiny of the White House, Capitol, and Supreme Court; of the great, green Mall with its monuments, memorials, and museums; of the Arlington bank of the Potomac, rich with memories of our wars.

The vista of the distant Mall extends along East Capitol Street (foreground), passing between the old Jefferson Building of the Library of Congress, with its green cupola, and the classic Supreme Court Building, erected in the 1930s. Until then the justices met in the Capitol. The other green-roofed building, at left, is the Library's first annex, the Adams Building. Beside it, the smaller Folger Shakespeare Library offers a charming site for scholars of the Bard.

Symbol for all America, the Capitol with its mighty dome dominates Washington. But the great building had a turbulent youth—burned by a British task force in retaliation for the burning of York (now Toronto) in Canada. Rebuilt, it sprouted like a teenager, quickly outgrowing its dome, finally getting a new one, even while the Civil War raged. President Lincoln insisted that the sight of it completed would reassure the people that their nation was here to stay.

Washington stretches northward to distant Maryland, its foreground slashed by the Mall. This green sward, sometimes called the Capitol's lawn, is flanked here by Smithsonian museums: the old red "Castle" and its superb garden, the discreet Freer Gallery, the outrageously Victorian Arts and Industries Building, and the round Hirshhorn Museum. Other museums lie across the Mall. Those red tile roofs indicate government buildings.

The Castle, the original Smithsonian Building, faces the Museum of Natural History across the Mall. Beneath that formal garden, two museums display African and Eastern art. Enter through those twin pavilions and go down 60 feet. Lincoln climbed the flag tower with the first Smithsonian secretary, Joseph Henry, to watch his troops at semaphore drill.

Union Station, grand architectural bow
to ancient Rome, opened in the early 1900s, when railroads ruled
much of the economy. The station served presidents, foreign heads of
state, and thousands of wartime servicemen. Its importance ebbed
with train travel, but it's been fully restored as an arcade of chic shops
and eateries and, once again, a busy station.

ABOVE

The Holocaust Museum, one of the city's newest,
tells movingly the terrible story of the Nazi concentration
camps. The rounded entrance is on 14th Street.

LEFT

National Gallery of Art, with blank walls and
pearl-like dome, stands on the north side of the Mall.
Its collection of Old Masters was a gift to the nation from
the millionaire Andrew Mellon. It opened in 1941.

Aiming at the Capitol, old Maryland Avenue
slices through northeast Washington according to L'Enfant's
plan. Simple row houses line the streets of this section, all rela-
tively new, for Upper Northeast, as this is called, long
remained less built-up than other sections of the District. In
the background rise government and private office buildings.

LEFT

Pennsylvania Avenue arrows
past the Department of Justice and the
tower of the Old Post Office on its way
from Capitol to White House, just as
L'Enfant planned. Scene of countless
parades, from the two-day march-past of
the Union Army in 1865 to the traditional
folklore of inauguration days with school-
boy bands and dancing pom-pom girls,
prancing politicians on horseback, and the
ruler-straight gray lines from West Point.
The old avenue has seen it all.

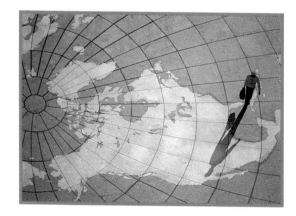

ABOVE

A busy Washington worker
steps on the Florida Keys as he traverses
the world's largest world map. The Navy
Memorial etches world geography onto a
Pennsylvania Avenue plaza 100 feet across.
A sculpture, "Lone Sailor" by Stanley
Bleifield, stands here along with four quiet
waterfalls in tribute to our Navy.

ABOVE

Washington Navy Yard, a shadow of its former self, lines the Anacostia with almost empty docks. The long brick build- ing is the old Naval Gun Factory, no longer needed. But the old base contains the splendid Naval museum.

LEFT

The Pentagon collects superlatives along with military brass. Still called the world's largest office building, covering 29 acres, it would be big enough to see on the moon through the Hale telescope. World War II demanded it, and it quickly rose across the Potomac from Washington—the perfect place to lose a troublesome general!

The Navy Medical Center in Bethesda, Maryland, *left,* looms over a grassy spread of land reaching to Wisconsin Avenue which is suitable for helicopters to use. They clattered here all night long on a November weekend in 1963—after the assassination of President John F. Kennedy. The Walter Reed Army Medical Center, *right,* near Rock Creek Park, honors the Army doctor who ended yellow fever, great killer of the Spanish-American War. Here, and at the Navy Medical Center, presidents go for checkups and humiliate themselves in hospital gowns just like everyone else. That's democracy.

Off Maryland's segment of
Wisconsin Avenue, nearly opposite the
Navy Medical Center, are the buildings
of the National Institutes of Health
(NIH). This is a research center, not a
hospital. The only patients are those
undergoing tests that will add to knowledge of disease control. Since Americans
pay for this establishment in taxes, the
NIH welcomes visitors. Orientation and
tours get them involved in the dramatic
war against disease. Doctors, of course,
come here frequently to keep current
with the new knowledge that
NIH provides.

LEFT

Phalanxes of white stones sweep through more than 600 gentle acres at Arlington National Cemetery, where lie some 230,000 Americans who fought in all the nation's wars. The lovely spread of Virginia hillside was once Robert E. Lee's estate, sacrificed when he refused to turn his sword against his homeland. The Custis-Lee House, built in 1802, gleams amidst the trees. Some of the Rebel soldiers lie here beside their old enemies, and their touching epitaph sums up why all Americans have fought for their country: "In simple obedience to duty as they understood it."

ABOVE

Giant bronze marines of World War II strive to raise their flag atop the volcanic peak of Suribachi—high point of an unforgettable island named Iwo Jima. Sculpted from a famous photograph, this is the Marine Corps War Memorial.

OVERLEAF

Jefferson Memorial shines beside the Tidal Basin. Virginia high-rises etch the horizon.

Willows weep beside the small lagoon
that flanks the Lincoln Memorial Reflecting Pool,
seen opposite. The Mall is rich in water—after all,
most of it was originally submerged.

LEFT

The Washington Monument erupts from its ring of fifty flags on the Mall. Begun in 1848, work on the project was halted by the Civil War. Building resumed a decade later, but a new quarry provided stone of a slightly different color. The line of demarcation is easy to spot. Those athletes who used to climb the 555-foot obelisk (no longer allowed) saw 188 inscribed stones, donated by states, foreign nations, and private groups.

RIGHT

The Mall's western end stretches to the tree-lined Reflecting Pool, bearing the image of the Lincoln Memorial. Washington Monument's shadow falls like the mark of a sundial on the green islet of the lagoon, *seen opposite at close range.*

LEFT

A westering sun highlights the monumental Mall: in the background, the west front of the Capitol; left of its huge cap, the dark dome of the Museum of Natural History; to the right of the Capitol, the green dome of the old Jefferson Building of the Library of Congress. In the center towers the Monument, partly mirrored by the Reflecting Pool. The rear of Lincoln Memorial fills the foreground with its simple Doric columns and friezes; state seals line its outer roof. In World War II, Maryland's seal was destroyed by gunfire. *Our* gunfire, that is. A GI manning Washington's defenses was apparently showing off to his girl.

And . . . oops!

Part Two

THE CAPITAL'S RESIDENTIAL BODY

Here is the body of the city, where it sleeps, works, eats, plays, studies, and prays. As capital of a melting-pot nation, Washington offers almost endless variations on those themes. Its people, of every ethnic and racial background, rich and poor, triumphant and defeated, find room to practice their life styles. Here lies Georgetown beside the Potomac, rolling from the distant Piedmont. Older than the city that now engulfs it, this is home to the very rich, also the struggling student, the hustling lawyer, and the wastrel haunting the entrance to a splendid restaurant.

From the barrel vault of Union Station, at right, famed Massachusetts Avenue heads for distant Dupont Circle and, beyond that, the tree-shaded mansions of Embassy Row. Some 150 embassies, counting those on circles and offshoots of the avenue, cling close to that area. Just before crossing Rock Creek Park the broad avenue slips by the discreet Japanese Embassy where, on December 7, 1941, smoke rose from burning records. Then, climbing toward the National Cathedral, "Mass Ave" passes the brilliant Islamic Center, a transplanted slice of the Moslem world with soaring minarets and bright mosaic designs. After that comes the British Embassy, a fine Georgian "Great Home," where all society vies for an invitation during a royal visit.

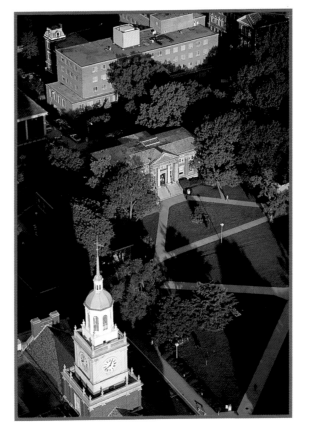

ABOVE

Howard University was founded right after the Civil War by one-armed General Oliver O. Howard, who had been appointed head of the Freedmen's Bureau. Many former slaves joined its student body and, though open to all, Howard remains predominantly African-American. Ralph Bunche and Thurgood Marshall were graduates, as is Andrew Young.

LEFT

Slender spires point out Georgetown, oldest American Roman Catholic University. John Carroll, of Maryland's eminent Catholic family, founded it two years before L'Enfant produced his plan for the capital. The original Old North Building still stands. Famous for law and medical schools—the latter running a noted hospital—GU's foreign service program is first and largest in the nation.

The painted dome and spire of the National Shrine of the Immaculate Conception, a landmark seen for miles, points out the northeast section of the District of Columbia and also Catholic University, which sponsored the National Shrine. CU is famous for its school of drama, one of the world's best.

Since Teddy Roosevelt laid its foundation, Washington National Cathedral took nearly a century to complete. But while work on its transepts continued, while stone carvers shaped finials and glaziers assembled stained glass, services continued wherever a roof permitted. President Wilson lies here; so does Helen Keller. And a moon rock was included in a stained glass window.

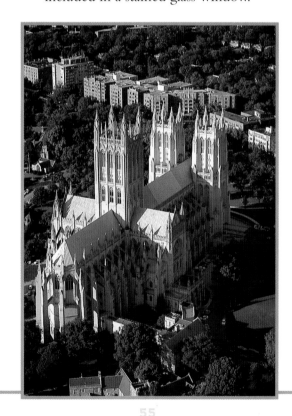

Georgetown's waterfront was loading hands of tobacco aboard colonial ships before the capital had been envisioned. And now again, Georgetown has a waterfront—a development that would boggle the eyes of those early planters. This multiuse structure is called Washington Harbour. Outdoor tables offer a view of rowing races—more fun than the cement plant that used to rattle away here.

LEFT

Another piece of modern architecture is the Intelsat Building heading out Connecticut Avenue. It houses a complex of satellite communication labs, and from above resembles a "Star Trek" spaceship with skylit atria and insulated offices.

OVERLEAF

Dupont Circle, where Massachusetts and Connecticut Avenues meet New Hampshire Avenue and P Street, makes more sense from the air than from a car. Traffic bewilders even the old-timers, but the circle, with its fountain and greenery, is a pleasant spot and the focus of social mix—once elegant, sometimes dowdy, later youthful.

LEFT

Tell a taxi driver "Georgetown," and you'll be delivered to this corner, marked by the gilt dome of a branch of the Riggs National Bank. Here M Street, coming from lower right, crosses Wisconsin Avenue, climbing past Dumbarton Oaks toward the National Cathedral on the horizon. On Halloween, or after a big Redskins victory, avoid this heart of Georgetown. It's a mess.

BELOW

Benjamin Stoddert, friend of George Washington and first Secretary of the Navy, built Georgetown's Halcyon House in the 1780s. A large front section (with flag) was later added by Mark Twain's nephew. The complex was recently restored, and art studios built under the rectangular garden.

Above lies another intersection, 18th Street and Columbia Road, that marks a neighborhood—Adams-Morgan. Named for two schools that integrated, the area has drawn Latin Americans, West Indians, and Africans to mix with native whites and African-Americans. The ethnic stew is tasty, as restaurants and an autumn street fair attest. Built mostly at the turn of the twentieth century, Adams-Morgan's residential streets, *left,* are rich with trees. Shops and diverse restaurants line 18th Street, *right*. Since becoming trendy in recent years, the neighborhood has seen an increase in prices, and bargains aren't what they used to be.

Famous Connecticut Avenue crosses Calvert Street after both bridge the winding Rock Creek. Passing famous hotels like the Shorham and its apartments, at left, Connecticut Avenue arrows straight toward Chevy Chase and the border of Maryland's wealthy Montgomery County. The avenue stays beside Rock Creek Park, and the park abruptly takes in the National Zoo, part of the Smithsonian, where science and display meet. Despite setting many records in the breeding of endangered animals, the zoo's veterinarians had no luck getting America's famous pandas, Hsing-Hsing and Ling-Ling, to raise a family.

Escalators plunge far underground to serve
Washington's Metro. It's an ultramodern subway system,
well run, comfortable and efficient, with color-coded lines
and quiet cars. Washingtonians are rightly proud of it.
This station is near the National Archives.

Historic flags with different styles and numbers
of stars fly above the Pennsylvania Avenue sidewalk outside
the J. Edgar Hoover Building. This home of the FBI is a stark,
forbidding fortresslike structure that Washingtonians quickly
dubbed "Fort Hoover."

LEFT

This huge aviary is one of many delights
at the National Zoological Park, full name of the zoo.
Migrating birds flying over Rock Creek Park often drop in near
here to touch base with distant cousins. The zoo really started
with gifts of live creatures to the Smithsonian. Its small herd of
bison used to graze on the Mall beside the Castle. Spurred by
Theodore Roosevelt and other naturalists, the zoo was set up
in Rock Creek Park in 1891 and has grown strong in its
research on saving and breeding rare species.

OVERLEAF

Seward Johnson's "The Awakening" fascinates
youngsters at Hains Point, jutting between the river and the
Washington Channel. The "buried" giant, apparently rising
from the ground, is a composition of five separate aluminum
sculptures, that mark the cleaning up of the "dead" Potomac

OVERLEAF

No statement about Washington is complete without a cheer for its professional football team, the fabled Redskins. Even when they're having a lousy season—which seldom happens—their stadium, a memorial to Robert F. Kennedy, is jammed with fans. In a city with racial and economic tensions, their frequent successes, their marching band in feathered headdress hammering out their splendid fight song, their *glamor,* knits together all factions.

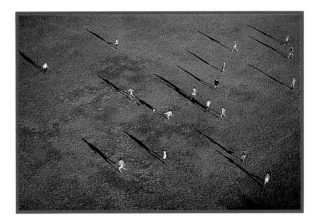

ABOVE

Soccer players take over a Washington park. Pickup teams may play at lunchtime; offices have baseball teams; many embassies stage cricket matches.

RIGHT

In the Potomac this 88-acre sanctuary for wild birds, beavers, foxes, and old forest trees lures nature lovers. It's named, of course, for our naturalist-president, Theodore Roosevelt, whose statue by Paul Manship stands in the clearing. Roosevelt Island is accessible by footbridge or canoe. That's Key Bridge in the background, with Georgetown behind it and the cathedral on the horizon.

LEFT

The Washington marina, where scores of "live-aboards" dwell in a floating neighborhood of close commuters—quick to notify each other of household leaks.

RIGHT

For years every visitor wanted to see the Watergate Hotel and apartments. Here it is: a curving complex of balconies with the big, rectangular Kennedy Center looming behind. The other building in the foreground is the Howard Johnson Motor Inn where lookouts could spy into the Democratic Party headquarters, and from which was launched the burglary attempt that finally forced President Nixon to resign—our greatest political scandal.

RIGHT

Morning traffic from Virginia blends at Roosevelt Bridge, which nips the end of Roosevelt Island on the way into Washington.

BELOW

An eight-oared shell coasts, oars dragging to steady it, as the coach motors alongside. Virginia high school crews, rowing on the Potomac, are good enough to rate frequent invitations to England's Henley regatta.

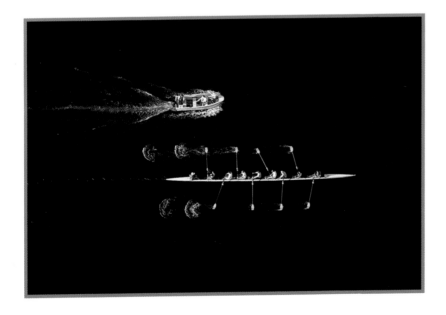

LEFT

Twining, traffic-smothered highways bring a clog of commuters onto the Capital Beltway—a 60-odd-mile loop around the District of Columbia. Washington's Metro—here above ground—slides serenely past.

RIGHT

Metro's sleek cars, unadorned by spray-paint graffiti, cool their wheels in a yard, awaiting the call for rush hour.

Part Three

THE CAPITAL'S NEIGHBORHOOD

Critics of the City of Washington—and there have been thousands of them—have complained that it was a malarial swamp, a cultural desert, a climatic catastrophe. The British Embassy at one time outraged Washington society by giving its staff hardship pay and "hill leave" —a term used in India to describe getting away from tropical heat and humidity. Today the swamps are filled, the mosquitoes killed off, and culture thrives. Families have found delight in the Maryland and Virginia countryside and the rural stretches of the Potomac. Little wonder George Washington doted on his riverside estate, Mount Vernon, with its acres of varied woodlands and fields of scientifically farmed crops. Among world capitals, ours is now considered fortunate for the natural beauty around it.

LEFT

Fort Washington, originally named Fort Warburton, rose as an earthen breastwork on the Potomac's Maryland shore when George Washington picked the site to guard the river. A lot of good it did in 1814! When a British task force approached on the way upriver, the American garrison skedaddled and left a clear route to the capital. The British set fire to the fort, then burned the government buildings of Washington. Rebuilt by Pierre L'Enfant and subsequently renamed, Fort Washington did its job in the Civil War and now makes a fine place for a picnic.

BELOW

This wild wetland draws nature lovers. It's the Dyke Marsh, flanking the Potomac and stretching beside George Washington Parkway South of Alexandria en route to Mount Vernon.

An excursion boat heads downstream past Alexandria, on the way to Mount Vernon. Returning upstream, passengers get a distant view of the nation's capital, its buildings gleaming on the horizon, the white shaft of the Washington Monument unmistakable from miles away. Between the city and Alexandria lies National Airport.

A pleasant new waterfront rims the Potomac shore of Alexandria.
Boutiques, restaurants, and restored buildings await the sailors who step ashore.

RIGHT

In 1922, members of the Alexandria Masonic Lodge broke ground for the
George Washington Masonic National Memorial. The 333-foot tower, which houses
much memorabilia of the lodge's famous member, is visible for miles.

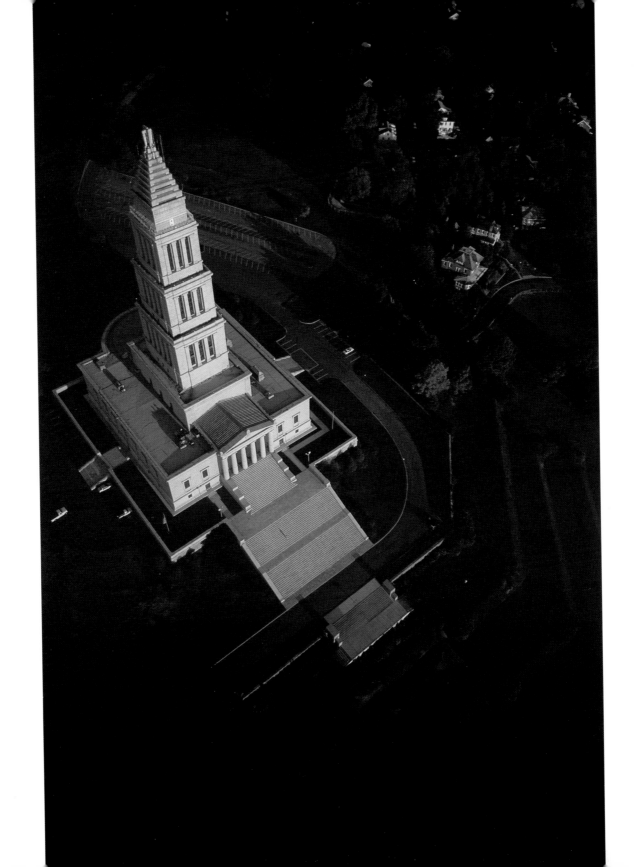

LEFT

This part of Old Town Alexandria is a long way from old. These are ultramodern offices and plants that benefit from the address and also from the trees and open parks.

BELOW

Old Town Alexandria has been restored to its eighteenth-century look, though well-heeled government staffers live in many of its townhouses. Still, a few street cobbles and fine tree-shaded homes would make George Washington feel comfortable visiting his old haunts—as they say he does.

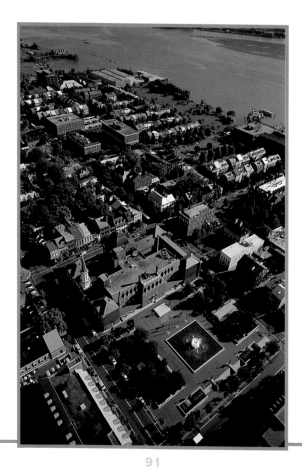

Washington National
Airport opened in 1941,
a model of modern
convenience. It's now
overcrowded, its air traffic
heavy and noisy as it thunders
over the river, its ground
traffic impossible. Congress
loves the place because it
offers convenient parking for
members. Others await
improvements.

Woodrow Wilson Bridge carries the Capital Beltway across the Potomac south of Alexandria. It's a drawbridge, going up (with plenty of warning to commuters) for occasional tall ships that come to visit, to in turn be visited by hordes of schoolchildren.

Crystal City, on the Virginia side of the river, near National Airport, modern with slick new high-rise hotels and office buildings. It's served by the Metro.

BELOW

With broad sidewalks for pedestrian sightseers, Memorial Bridge points straight at Arlington Cemetery and the distant Custis-Lee mansion. The bridge starts at the Lincoln Memorial, where a similar vista, the two-mile–long Mall, heads to the Capitol.

LEFT

High-rises dominate Rosslyn, in Virginia. Washington, just across the river, hasn't allowed them. They're higher than the statue on the dome of the Capitol!

OVERLEAF

At Great Falls, the Potomac tumbles from piedmont to tidewater in a thrashing turmoil of white water. After this awesome display, the river rolls on, innocently sedate, past the nation's capital.

RIGHT

Wolf Trap Farm Park has brought top-notch opera stars, bluegrass singers, comedians, and dance groups to delight Washingtonians. The huge wooden concert hall in the Virginia countryside holds 3,500 people, while 3,000 more risk the weather on the grass outside.

BELOW

A glimpse of the twenty-first century in the Virginia countryside—the Xerox Center. It's an international complex for training, a small city in itself, population about 1,000, with every amenity as well as the training areas. The whole facility, near historic Leesburg, covers more than 100 acres.

Thomas Jefferson's Monticello is worth the 120-mile drive from Washington southwestward to Charlottesville, Virginia. The home that he designed, built, furnished, rebuilt, tinkered with, improved upon for 40 years, and loved with all his heart, stands on a hill just southeast of the town. It's been beautifully kept; restoration of the land and outbuildings continues, just as Jefferson would have wished—except that he would have doubtless made some changes along the way. Here are a mass of inventions and innovations—insulation for winter, a cooling process for summer, a desk surface that turns like a lazy Susan, a series of joined pens that copy several letters at once—dozens of small gadgets that could only flow from a mind ever seeking the betterment of mankind.

LEFT

Virginia horse country. Rolling meadows near Middleburg sweep from the Blue Ridge to the Potomac. Here the gentry still ride to hounds, and the ghosts of Jeb Stuart's Rebel cavalry still linger.

At historic Harper's Ferry the Shenandoah meets the Potomac among the steep, forested slopes of the Appalachian range. Here in 1859 John Brown raided, trying to spark a slave revolt. He was captured by U.S. Marines led by an army colonel named Robert E. Lee.

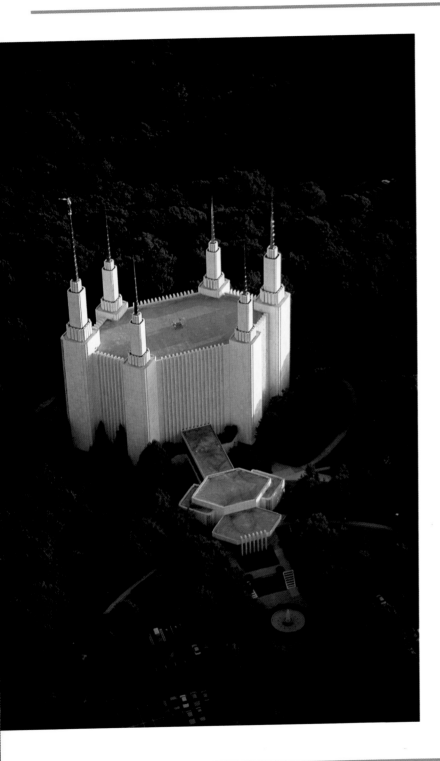

LEFT

Only Mormons can enter their spectacular but secluded temple just off the Capital Beltway in Kensington, Maryland. That's the Angel Moroni, gold-plated atop the highest spire.

RIGHT

With barely a glance at the autumn foliage, rush-hour commuters cram the outer loop of the Beltway between Maryland suburbs of Silver Spring and Bethesda. Built in the sixties, the 60-mile route around the city eased downtown traffic for a while. But the cars soon caught up.

Above-ground Metro stations are easy to spot from the air because of their tubular roofs. The one above serves Silver Spring, Maryland, not an incorporated town, but a Washington suburb with new office buildings and malls, *left*.

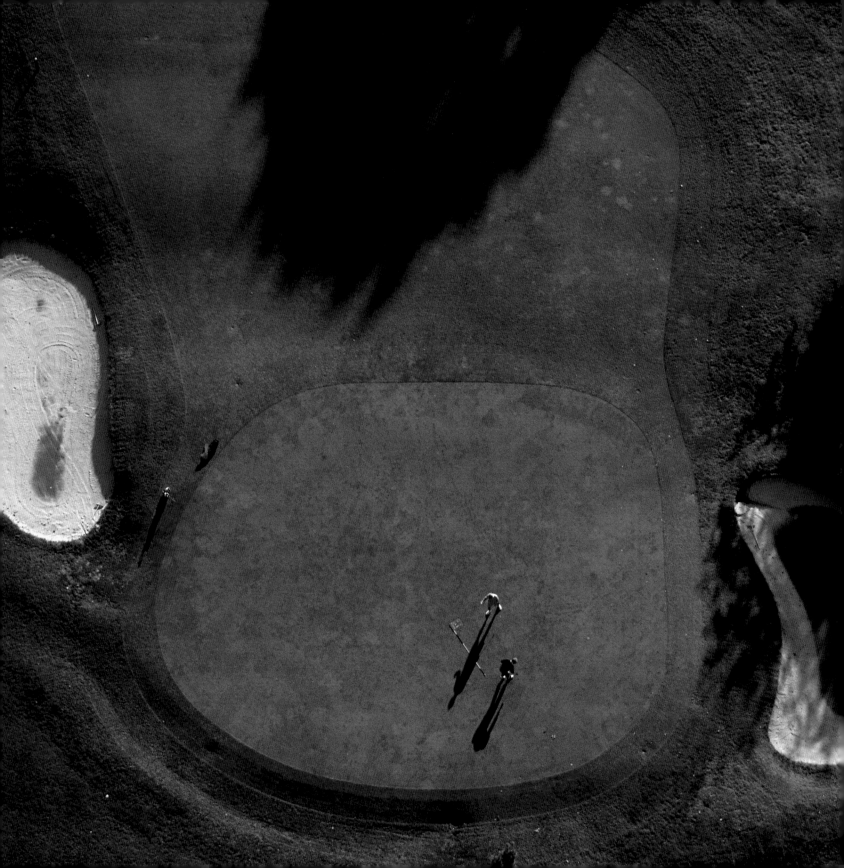

LEFT

Chevy Chase and Bethesda are affluent suburbs in Maryland, with famous golf courses such as Congressional, Columbia, and Burning Tree, where President Eisenhower was a regular.

RIGHT

A canal to link rich western lands to ocean shipping was George Washington's dream. At last the Chesapeake and Ohio Canal was built from Georgetown to Cumberland, Maryland, 185 miles away. For more than 20 miles in the District and suburban Maryland, the old C&O takes passengers in canal boats. Bikers can follow the towpath the whole distance.

Beautifully engineered, the five-mile Chesapeake Bay Bridge bears heavy traffic on summer weekends as hordes of Washingtonians head for Ocean City, Rehobeth, and other Atlantic beach resorts.

Fog shrouds the Patuxent
River near Upper Marlboro,
Maryland, where colonial
families once rolled hogsheads
of tobacco to river wharves
for shipment to England.
Many old homes still stand
here; also rolling roads.

Chesapeake shorelines are often too spongy for human intrusion. But marshes and meanders are rich in herons, egrets, ospreys, and winter's skeins of Canada geese and swans.

Environmental scientists study such wetlands, testing for pollutants in the runoff streams and the effects that human intrusions have on the burgeoning life of isolated waterways.

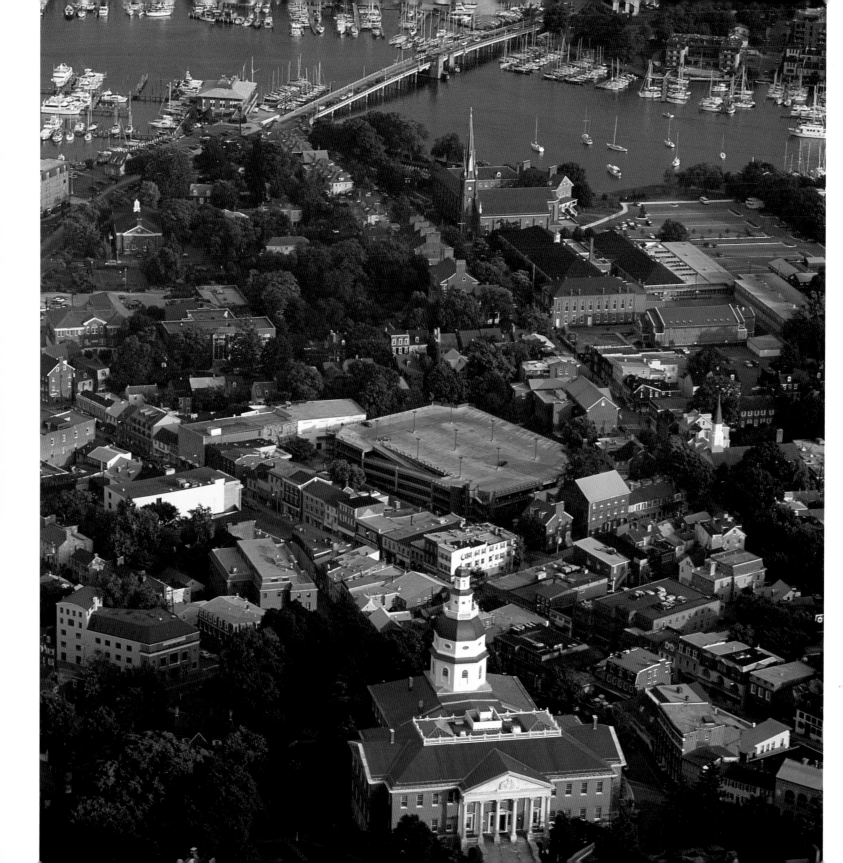

LEFT

Annapolis, Maryland's capital, has scores of eighteenth-century houses still in use along lane-like streets. The domed State Capitol served as the national Capitol for a few months during the pre-Washington era. General Washington resigned his commission here.

ABOVE

Annapolis is famous as a sailing capital and also as home of the U.S. Naval Academy. The huge central gray building is Bancroft Hall, where some 4,000 midshipmen have their rooms. Classroom buildings and labs train minds; playing fields harden bodies.

LEFT

A cutter-rigged sailboat slips out of a huge
Annapolis marina for a weekend exploring the Chesapeake's
"gunkholes"—small inlets and coves where a family can
anchor for a peaceful night afloat. Boat traffic is now
so great that every sailor knows every gunkhole.

OVERLEAF

Low sun gilds the ripples as a breeze stirs the South River,
near Annapolis, and hurries three sailboats on their way.

Little wonder the capital's founders were drawn to the Potomac.
Though it has its share of youthful escapades in the distant hills, it's grown serene in middle
age as it passes here, near Leesburg. The river's crashing drop at Great Falls is yet to come.

After that, mellowed by experience, it flows sedately through Washington and on to the bay.
The river, turbulent, then small and smug, facing thundering crisis, then reaching massive
grandeur, seems to mirror the city which chose its shore as its birthplace.

A free exchange is all it is. Of

words and ideas, facts and figures,

hopes, dreams and opportunities.

Communication.

Through our technology, we

provide the means to communicate.

And through our participation in

organizations and events, we help

provide the opportunity for people

to better understand each other.

⊕ Bell Atlantic